In MEMORY of my BELOVED.

Birthdate: _____
Adoption Date: _____
Departure Date: _____

Add Photo Here

Dear Pet Lover,

I want to start by expressing my sympathies for what you are going through right now. I know first hand what it feel like to lose a dear companion and it is for this reason I want to share a tool to help you celebrate their life and mourn their loss from the physical world.

Working through grief can be challenging and it can take time. This journal is designed to help relieve some of the weight you feel from the loss of your beloved pet. It can also be used as a tool to help you prepare for that final day if you have an aging or sick pet.

As you reminisce and reflect on all you've gained from your time with them you can also start to open to the future that is possible because of them. Our pets are often some of our greatest teachers, best friends, and soul guiding companions.

The journaling process can help your body, mind and heart soothe and recalibrate. It will allow you to get in touch with your emotions rather than bury them inside causing more trouble and pain. The journal you build with memories, photos, and other unique details about them will become a treasured keepsake for years to come. It will also be a useful aid when grief rises again on anniversary, holidays, or other special dates you shared.

TIPS FOR USING THIS BOOK

- **Take your time.** Work through this book at your own pace.
- **Be gentle with yourself.** Grief is not a linear process and doesn't look the same for everyone. Move through this journal and exercises in a way that is supportive for you. If you want to skip a section because you aren't ready to focus on that area, come back to it when you are ready.
- **Review this book when you are missing your beloved pet.**
- **Share it with family members** so they can support your healing process or perhaps receive assistance of their own.
- This journal is meant to move with you through the grief journey which means you may complete most of it and then **come back and write again in 6 months or a year or two later.**
- There are specific areas set aside for writing and adding pictures but don't feel confined by those prompts. **Get creative. This book should reflect you.** Make it your own by adding drawings, poems, photos, or other mementos where you see fit.
- **Many blank lined pages have been added at the back** so if any prompt inspires more words than the allotted lines allow, use the extra writing spaces to capture your thoughts & feelings.
- **Coloring can be a helpful mindfulness activity**. Add color to the drawings throughout the book to help you center yourself.

"Until one has loved an animal, a part of one's soul remains unawakened." - Anatole France

REMEMBERING HOW WE MET...

How I found you..

_____

_____

_____

I knew you were the right one for me when...

_____

_____

_____

_____

I remember feeling...

_____

_____

_____

_____

The day I brought you home...

_____

_____

_____

_____

SOME OF OUR FIRST MOMENTS TOGETHER

Add photos

Things you loved...

Things you didn't like...

Something that always brings a smile to my face is...

Lets go!

Places we liked to walk...

People we liked to visit

Animals we loved to see

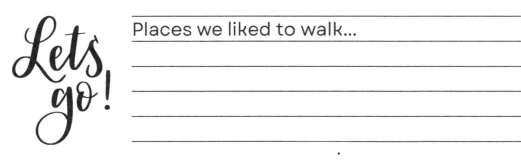

Favorites trips we took together...

OUR ADVENTURES

Add photos

People would often say this about you...

_____
_____
_____
_____
_____
_____
_____
_____

When I would get home you would...

_____
_____
_____
_____
_____
_____

Your favorite spot in the house was...

_____
_____
_____
_____
_____
_____
_____

HOME IS WHERE YOUR HEART IS

Add photos

You'd let me know what you wanted by...

_____

_____

_____

_____

Your special talent was...

_____

_____

_____

_____

_____

_____

_____

_____

_____

_____

What made our relationship unique was...

_____

_____

_____

_____

_____

Other Memories I want to capture are....

xoxo

Other Memories I want to capture are....

forever

Other Memories I want to capture are....

_____

_____

_____

_____

_____

_____

_____

_____

_____

_____

_____

_____

_____

_____

_____

_____

_____

_____

Other Memories I want to capture are....

_____

_____

_____

_____

_____

_____

_____

_____

_____

_____

_____

_____

_____

_____

_____

_____

_____

_____

_____

Add photos

you♡me

Add photos

Feeling your Emotions

"What we once enjoyed and deeply loved we can never lose, for all that we love deeply becomes part of us." - Helen Keller

There is no timeframe for your grief. Everyone needs to go through their process in their own pace. The important thing is that you are doing the work to move forward and getting additional help when you need it.

We create a special bond with our pets because for many they are the one being that loved us unconditionally and we could also love unconditionally in return. It is likely they opened your heart and healed you in ways that you didn't expect.

It is important to take time to consciously go through this grieving process so that your heart can one day be ready to welcome a new companion into your life again.

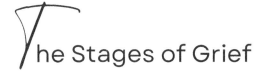

The Stages of Grief

There are six main stages of grief commonly used to define the process and often many more emotions felt outside of that framework. The concept of the stages of grief was introduced by psychiatrist Elisabeth Kübler-Ross and they have been adapted by many since. The stages are not linear. You may move through them in different orders and return to certain stages many times.

Denial

It can be often hard to believe your pet is gone. This can be especially true if their passing was sudden or unexpected. You may find yourself calling them for dinner or expecting to see them in their favorite spot. Be gentle with yourself. It can take time to adjust to the fact they are aren't physically with you now.

Anger

As you try to accept their passing, anger may surface. We look to blame others or even ourselves for their death. You may feel mad at the circumstances that led to their passing or even point fingers at other people even though it isn't their fault. In some way our mind is trying to make sense or give reason for this pain we feel.

Bargaining

This stage you may find yourself exploring the 'what if' scenarios - what if I had taken them for a check up sooner or what if I we hadn't gone on that trip. You are yearning to turn back time so their passing doesn't occur. This can also include bargaining with a higher power and making some sort of offer in exchange for their life back. Our mind is looking for a solution to the pain we feel and trying to regain power in a situation we feel no control.

Depression

Deep sadness can become depression as their passing is accepted and the emptiness their departure left is felt. It's common to move through a deep sadness state during this realization. It is important to seek support if this sadness becomes a depressed state you cannot seem to move through.

Acceptance

Here you have begun to live with their loss and are gradually moving forward in living your life without them. You are starting to integrate your memories of them in a way that allows you to continue on with life.

Finding Meaning

In this stage you are reflecting on the meaning your relationship had and the purpose it served in your life. You open to honoring their memory in a way that reflects who they were and how they impacted your life.

NOTICE WHAT STAGES YOU ARE EXPERIENCING RIGHT NOW.

Recognizing what emotions you are feeling and how they may be part of the grieving process can be helpful in making sense of your experience of life right now. Both positive & negative emotions are normal during this time. Numbness - not feeling anything - can be common too. It is your body's way of protecting you from feeling overloaded. Which of these are you feeling now?

Lonely

Abandoned   Shocked   Unfocused

Anger

Distracted   Irritable

Sad

Anxious

Guilt   Overwhelmed

Worried

Relief

Frustration   Hopeless

Regretful   Surprised

Disconnected   Needy

Disillusionment   Happy   Sadness

Gratitude   Yearning   Disappointed

Calm

Hopeful   Supported   Scared

Journaling about your emotions is a supportive way to help you understand and process feelings. Use the next few pages - daily, monthly, yearly - as often as you need to express your thoughts and feelings about your beloved pet's passing. Unresolved feelings have a way of continuing to negatively impact our lives so allow yourself to feel fully what your body wants to release.
(Note: There are more blank pages at the back of the journal.)

Date _____

_____

_____

_____

_____

_____

_____

_____

_____

_____

_____

_____

_____

_____

_____

_____

_____

My heart is big enough to hold both love and pain.

Date _____

_____

_____
_____
_____
_____
_____
_____
_____
_____
_____
_____
_____
_____
_____
_____
_____
_____
_____
_____
_____
_____

I am more resilient than I know.

Date _____

_____

_____
_____
_____
_____
_____
_____
_____
_____
_____
_____
_____
_____
_____
_____
_____
_____
_____
_____
_____
_____
_____
_____

Each day my heart heals a little more.

Date _____

_____

I am taking small steps towards healing everyday.

Date _____

_____

I am allowing myself the time and space needed to grieve.

Date _____

_____

_____
_____
_____
_____
_____
_____
_____
_____
_____
_____
_____
_____
_____
_____
_____
_____
_____
_____
_____
_____

I give myself permission to feel a range of emotions.

Date _____

_____

_____

_____

_____

_____

_____

_____

_____

_____

_____

_____

_____

_____

_____

_____

_____

_____

_____

_____

_____

_____

_____

_____

_____

I am open to finding joy in the small moments of life even now as I grieve.

Date _____

Getting Support

"Don't cry because it's over, smile because it happened." - Dr. Seuss

Connect with Others

Everyone goes through grief in their own way. Some naturally lean into others for comfort and can talk about what they're going through openly. Other people find they need more alone time to process their thoughts and emotions in private.

Be careful alone time doesn't become isolation. Having face-to-face connection with others is important to the healing process.

Grief can be uncomfortable for others because they don't have experience with it themselves or don't know what to do or say. Let them know what you need - a shoulder to cry on, someone to chat with, or even just a hang out buddy. Just being with others that care about you is helpful.

Joining a **Grief Support Group** can also be immensely helpful when you don't have family or friends to lean on or if you need more support than they can provide. Joining with others going through loss similar to yours can help.

Seek out a **Grief Counsellor or Therapist** when you are feeling stuck or the emotions are too much to handle on your own.

What I need most right now is...

_____

_____

_____

_____

_____

_____

Remind yourself of friends & family you can call on for support.
List them here:

_____

_____

_____

_____

_____

_____

Contact info of a grief support group, therapist, or helpline
numbers you can reach out to if needed.

_____

_____

_____

_____

_____

_____

Saying Goodbye

"When you are sorrowful, look again in your heart, and you shall see that, in truth, you are weeping for that which has been your delight." - Kahlil Gibran

Creating a tribute or memorial ceremony is a great way to honor your beloved pet and is a therapeutic way to get a sense of closure after their death. Make it personal to you and your pet. Consider what aspects of their essence/personality would you like to celebrate. Here are a few things to consider:

- **Choose a location** that is meaningful to you and them. This may be your backyard, a favorite off leash park or maybe so other location that holds special significance or memories for you.
- **Consider who you would like to attend.** This would be family or friends that were close to you and your beloved pet.
- **Set a date and time** for the ceremony.
- **At the memorial space** you can include pictures or items that were special to your pet. Perhaps a favorite toy or treats they loved. You may like to include a candle, flowers, water, fire, maybe some favorite music, or any other elements that feel appropriate.
- **Prepare a personal tribute** you want to share and you can invite others to share any memories or thoughts they would like to offer in celebration of your beloved pet.

- **Have someone take a few photos** from the event. These memories can be added to this book as part of the keepsake tribute you are creating.
- **Make sure to allow time afterward**s for you and others to gather and continue to share with each other.
- **Consider creating a lasting memorial** that is meaningful to you that you can come back to when you need time to reflect on your beloved pet. This could be a bench, or planting a tree, or putting up some sort of plaque or chimes.

Creating a meaningful way to say goodbye is a supportive part of the grieving process. Make note of some of your ideas here:

_____

_____

_____

_____

_____

_____

_____

_____

_____

_____

_____

_____

TRIBUTE DAY MEMORIES

Add photos
& other mementos

A true love story never ends.

Daily Life Changes

"The world would be a nicer place if everyone had the ability to love as unconditionally as a dog." - M.K. Clinton

The loss of our beloved pet can be felt in multitude of ways throughout our day. This section is a place to reflect not only on what has changed and how it is affecting you, but also create new daily habits that can support this evolving time in your life.

How has their loss affected your daily life and routine?

_____

_____

_____

_____

_____

_____

_____

_____

Are there any unexpected ways their absence is felt?

_____

_____

_____

_____

_____

_____

_____

_____

What coping mechanisms, activities, or practices are you doing that help you navigate this daily change? (Ex. You still go for a walk around the block after work even without your pet by your side. Maybe you've taken up yoga to help you move the emotions in your body)

_____
_____
_____
_____
_____
_____
_____
_____
_____

How are other family members or pets coping with this change?

_____
_____
_____
_____
_____
_____
_____
_____
_____

CREATING A NEW ROUTINE

Our pets are often so much a part of our day. We can feel a little lost without them, especially when we are newly adjusting to their departure from our daily routines. It will be helpful to consciously create a new routine that includes self care activities that will support your grieving process.

List 5 things you can add to your morning routine

List 5 things you can add to your evening routine

Use the next few pages to journal about how the adjustment is going. Remember it can take time to get used to a new routine.

I am learning to connect with you and me in a new way.

Date _____

I am stronger with each day.

Date _____

_____

_____

_____

_____

_____

_____

_____

_____

_____

_____

_____

_____

_____

_____

_____

_____

_____

_____

_____

_____

_____

I can do this.

Date _____

_____

All you have taught me is forever in my heart and mind.

Date _____

_____

_____

_____

_____

_____

_____

_____

_____

_____

_____

_____

_____

_____

_____

_____

_____

_____

_____

_____

_____

The things we loved can still be the things I love.

It is ok to move forward.

Date _____

_____

_____

_____

_____

_____

_____

_____

_____

_____

_____

_____

_____

_____

_____

_____

_____

_____

_____

_____

_____

_____

_____

_____

You are always with me - even now.

Date _____

_____

_____

_____

_____

_____

_____

_____

_____

_____

_____

_____

_____

_____

_____

_____

_____

_____

_____

_____

_____

Soul Connections

"How lucky I am to have something that makes saying goodbye so hard." –Winnie The Pooh

If you think you and your pet had a special connection, it's true. Our pets choose us as much as we choose them. Our souls are here to help each other grow, heal, and open to our greatest potential. And although a pet will bond with the entire family in which they are raised, there is typically  one person in the family with whom they connect most deeply. My guess is that is you. And the reason why you are feeling their loss so deeply.

There are many who haven't yet opened their heart fully to an animal that would belittle this concept that our beloved pets came to help us in life. They might say they loved you because you were the one that fed them or were home more often. Don't let their limited awareness diminished your pet relationship and the sadness you feel from their passing. Perhaps one day they will have the blessing of experiencing this special soul connection with an animal and then they too will understand. Forgive their narrowminded comments as they just do not know yet what they do not know.

Our pets can teach us how to love unconditionally. They can show how to be patient, to ask for what we need, to be in the present moment, to play with our whole heart, and so many other things that will be specific to you and your journey in life. They will even help us with our physical and mental healing.

There are countless examples of people's pets who presented with the same physical illness or mental and emotional challenges as their beloved owner. They will mirror your vibration and as much as possible try to help you with your healing. Author Tammy Billups does a wonderful job describing this type of relationship in her book Animal Soul Contracts if you would like to read more. (There is no affiliation with this journal – just admiration for her work.)

Perhaps you are now wondering more about your soul connection with your beloved pet. Consider the questions on the following pages:

How were you and your pet's personalities the same?
And how did they differ?

_____

_____

_____

_____

_____

What did they teach you through your interactions?
(ex. Maybe you had to learn to be more patient)

_____

_____

_____

_____

_____

Did you and your beloved pet suffer any similar mental,
emotional or physical challenges? (ex. Maybe you both had
bladder issues or were shy around new people)

_____

_____

_____

_____

_____

At what point did they come into your life? Was there anything particularly challenging about that time or are you aware of anything you were needing? Chances are their presence was supportive in some way. (ex. Maybe you were just becoming an empty nester as the kids were all gone to school or perhaps another beloved pet had recently passed on.)

_____

_____

_____

_____

_____

_____

_____

_____

_____

_____

_____

_____

_____

_____

Gratitude

"When we think of those companions who travelled by our side down life's road, let us not say with sadness that they left us behind, but rather say with gentle gratitude that they once were with us."
–Unknown

Taking time to focus on gratitude can be a very healing part of your grief journey. It can fill and mend your heart in amazing ways.

Spend as much time as you need in this section. You can come back to it multiple times. As you journal, don't just list their qualities but write about specific stories, examples, or memories. This will make writing in this section most impactful to your healing as vibrations of love and gratitude flood your body.

What are you thankful your beloved pet showed you, shared, did, was by nature...

_____

_____

_____

_____

_____

_____

_____

_____

_____

_____

_____

_____

_____

_____

_____

_____

_____

_____

_____

_____

The lessons or qualities your pet brought into your life that you appreciate most are...

_____

_____

_____

_____

_____

_____

_____

_____

_____

_____

_____

_____

_____

_____

_____

_____

_____

_____

_____

_____

_____

Write a letter to your pet expressing your thoughts and feelings. What do you want them to know.

_____

_____

_____

_____

_____

_____

_____

_____

_____

_____

_____

_____

_____

_____

_____

_____

_____

_____

_____

_____

Keeping Memories Alive

"Dogs come into our lives to teach us about love, they depart to teach us about loss. A new dog never replaces an old dog, it merely expands the heart. If you have loved many dogs your heart is very big." –Erica Jong

To keep the memories of your beloved pet alive is to honor their impact on your life. It can help preserve the connection you shared and be comforting as you mourn their loss. Focusing on the joy and all the positive they brought to your life can help balance the negative emotions their absence brings.

Here a few ways to continue to celebrate their life and legacy.

- Share stories about them and their impact on your life with family and friends.
- Create a memory book – which is what you are doing here :)
- Frame a favorite photo to display.
- Have an artist draw or paint a portrait of your pet you can hang on your wall.
- Purchase or create a special memento in honor of them.
  Ex. clay paw print, unique jewelry piece, special urn
- Pull together a video montage of them.
- Establish a memorial fund or charity.
- Plant a memorial garden in their honor.
- Celebrate special dates – their birthday, adoption day & others.
- Volunteer at an animal shelter or consider fostering animals.
- Keep journaling about them as they come to mind and heart.

MOVING FORWARD

How would you like to continue to honor and remember them in meaningful ways?

_____

_____

_____

_____

_____

_____

_____

_____

Reflecting on their impact on your life, in what ways do you see their legacy living on? (Ex. Perhaps in how your treat your next beloved pet. In your desire to support other animal rescues.)

_____

_____

_____

_____

_____

_____

_____

_____

_____

How are you feeling about the moving forward step of the process?

_____

_____

_____

_____

_____

_____

_____

_____

_____

_____

_____

_____

_____

_____

_____

_____

_____

_____

_____

_____

_____

Add photos , drawings,
poems, etc

Signs from Beyond

"Never. We never lose our loved ones. They accompany us; they don't disappear from our lives. We are merely in different rooms." –Paulo Coelho

It is not unusual for people to still feel like they are connected to and receiving signs from their beloved pets once that have passed on.

Perhaps they appear to you in a dream.

Maybe you find a ball under their favorite tree in the park.

Maybe you thought you heard them bark, purr, or chirp.

They might send signs in the form of another animal or symbol that means something to you both.

Whether you believe in an afterlife or not, it is hard to deny the thousands of stories pet lovers have shared about connecting with their beloved animals after their departure from this physical world. If you are open to the possibilities, it is likely you will receive something from them.

What messages have your received from your beloved pet?

_____

_____

_____

_____

_____

_____

What signs or symbols have you noticed are an indication they are connecting with you?

_____

_____

_____

_____

_____

What messages would you like to receive from them. State it here and then pay attention to the signs you receive in response.

_____

_____

_____

_____

_____

_____

More Thoughts

"Pets teach us the purest kind of love." –Unknown

The following pages are for you to continue journaling through your grieving process without the guide and prompts. Sometimes it is helpful to just write freely what your mind and heart is needing to say.

Whether you make this a daily practice for a while or return to it when times are harder on birthdays and anniversaries, the choice is yours.

Remember the journey through loss of a beloved pet is one that is as unique as your relationship was with them. Move at your own pace. Come back to this journal and workbook as often as you need. You will be grateful for the beautiful keepsake you are building.

This journal/workbook is not a substitute for professional care. Seek a grief counsellor or therapist if you are struggling to cope.

I wish you much love and healing on your journey.

Date _____

Date _____

Date _____

Date _____

Date _____

Date _____

Date _____

Date _____

Date _____

Date _____

Date _____

Date _____

Date _____

Date _____

Date _____

Date _____

Date _____

Date _____

Date _____

Date _____

Date _____

Date _____

Date _____

Date _____

Date _____

Date _____

Date _____

Date _____

Date _____

Date _____

Date _____

Date _____

Date _____

Date _____

Date _____

Date _____

Date _____

Date _____

Date _____

Date _____

Date _____

Date _____

Date _____

Date _____

Date _____

Date _____

Date _____

Date _____

Date _____

Date _____

Date _____

This book was created by Conscious Minds Press.

Publisher of tools to help live a consciously
connected, healthy, and aware life. Journals,
Log books, Notebooks, Guides, Workbooks
and more to support you and those you love.

Please consider leaving us a review on Amazon.
Your positive feedback supports visibility of small
independent publishers like us and encourages
others to also invest in helpful tools for a
conscious & connected life.
(Find the book title in your order history or in
main search and click 'submit a product review'.)

Thank you kindly.

Made in the USA
Coppell, TX
13 July 2024

34584171R00077